CW00434286

HUMAN WORK

BY THE SAME AUTHOR

Bee Journal

HUMAN WORK

Sean Borodale

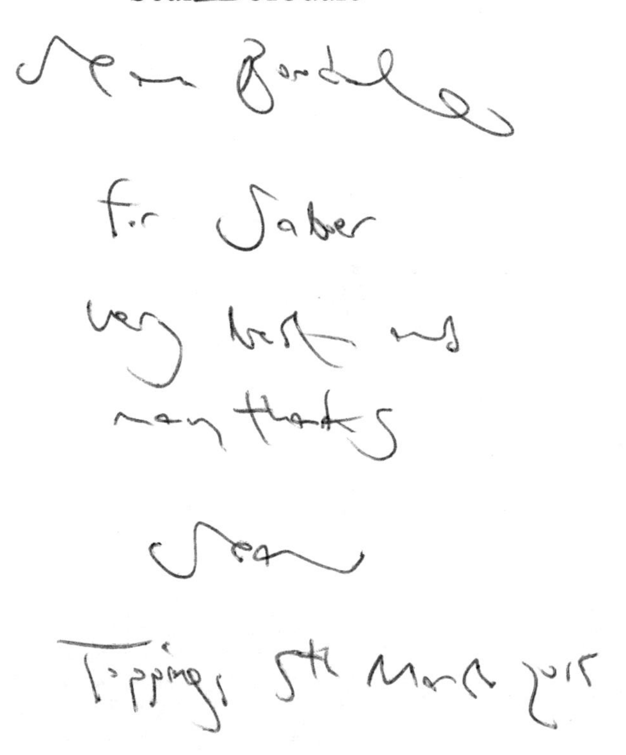

CAPE POETRY

Published by Jonathan Cape 2015

2 4 6 8 10 9 7 5 3 1

First published in Great Britain in 2015 by
Jonathan Cape
Random House, 20 Vauxhall Bridge Road,
London SW1V 2SA

www.randomhouse.co.uk

A Penguin Random House Company

Addresses for companies within The Random House Group Limited can be found at:
www.randomhouse.co.uk/offices.htm

The Random House Group Limited Reg. No. 954009

A CIP catalogue record for this book
is available from the British Library

ISBN 9780224099844

The Random House Group Limited supports the Forest Stewardship Council® (FSC®), the leading international forest-certification organisation. Our books carrying the FSC label are printed on FSC®-certified paper. FSC is the only forest-certification scheme supported by the leading environmental organisations, including Greenpeace. Our paper procurement policy can be found at www.randomhouse.co.uk/environment

Printed and bound in Great Britain by
CPI Group (UK) Ltd, Croydon CR0 4YY

Typeset by Palimpsest Book Production Ltd, Falkirk, Stirlingshire

the slight surprise of action

Bruno Latour

HUMAN WORK

I skin apples.

Like the flaying of Marsyas,
not tuneless
(but this is the noise);

bring the knife
towards the centre of the thumb,
flensing, in the factory of my hands

the living opened.

The inner canvas of their flesh
on the table's stage for dissection:
mute pale diagrams of anatomical apple.

I cut in, under the hide,
pressuring the blade into each core's
intrinsic barrel and battery of kin.

They sag in the pot's sweat, growing dislodged,
de-boned
to a hot, loose, wet, aggregate;

it bellows and blows:
a garden's agony I stir quiet,

riddling this tumbling dark with human work.

Washed jug,
scalded the muslin clean.

Took this heavy weeping,
this curd of crushed apple,

like it was a severed head wrapped in muslin.
[*I saw a fox.*]

Cupped hands (around its face),
squeezed with the thumbs;

worm-ends of mash scrolled through the mesh.

A trickle,
a spiral
filled
the jug;

liquid swerved pitch.
[*I heard a lark climb.*]

Washed hands,
rinsed a crabby, grey pollutant to the drains;
took curd to the compost, first frost.

We made a glassful, a clear-sided house
of cloudy, semi-precious strength;

it tasted old as the origin of apples.

I give this juice to you,
its slow-grown, slow-crushed
effort of handling;

hands foolish or touched, a Midas's gift.

We raised a toast to our makeshift apparatus,
true to attempting purpose;

found in its drinkable dignity, a depth:
the extracted oddness of the edible.

This pan of fruit is our workbench crucible's
elastic muscle of boiling liquor:
fruit, sugar, water [*in the language of sugar*].

When you're making a jam
there's a strange, turnable weather:
down there could twist into anything.

At the stove's furious station
(like a spinning-top wobbling on and on),

its concentrating conglomerate
transforms, more slow, more long

as the flame continues under its flatulence and burping,
viscous and constant.

I watch, test the strength of its set [*in the language of pectin*]
by the cold-plate technique, a spoon tilted to decant.

Some sovereign of the underworld appears,
coined in its profile

wrinkled on the jellied depth;
a hybrid of Hades and Persephone's – dead-knot fruit
dredged from the pan's dark.

For a moment I stand, strange in the tunic of window-light,
and feel weighted
over the ancient edge of a deathbed –
wind stopped, no race
just the flipside, the face in the crown:
king ruling an aeon for a second.

I touch its event of resistance, its frowning wet tack;
push the badge of the cold skin
and it shutters, warps, worries
like sandbars the sea has crossed; a flicker, concordance
with a set-point.

[*Done: take off the heat.*]

A heaviness wanders through the pan.
I scrape the scum, bottle

a generation of jam's dialect –
this year's mysterious wind, hedge, berry, broken flesh –

and ask,
is this body ever at peace, is it ever perfect?

I was asking, *is a body ever at peace?*

Like, how does it look to be stewed
until a skin develops an absence of flesh?
Pressed through the gauze of a wire mesh,
stripped of seed, boiled old with sugar
[*granulated, refined: do not burn*];

like, how does it look
whose creepy lack of minerals sets it searching:
gel-coloured torchlight, *grandmother sweets*.
Whatever fruit is, pressing its fidget to set-point;
ingredient of pectin working.

(Grim tales of utterly deformed woods
derange on the scum.)

Only the exosphere of a garden,
bubbling up time: the alembic miracle of the kitchen.

Test on a cold spoon the hot, sly, wild juice
snared in the syrup.

I have only this medium of result:
stickier on my hands, weirdly comforting.

It boils on, it lifts up and down on the puckering distress,
signals what kind of interrogation this is.

There is not even solitude in scrubbing potatoes.
The sound of the brush, the prising of eyes:
its sombre business.

There is not even solitude in the cutting of potatoes:
the starch on the knife,
the pale flesh from invisible fields.

They are the gloomy dead, potatoes,
along the walls at Mycenae.
Washed in the water the moon has moved –
the lap of flow, the lap of ebb.

Gingerbread gloom; I gather home.

While the last wasp, defiant,
enters and leaves the snow shape of mountains,
among trees, the painted woods, the tall pines
and the spruce, and the North's winter,
the North's visor, lowers, inspires ingredients:

I have Hansel-and-Gretel's prayer
searching the whereabouts of tracks, routes out.
I make time do.
Old mother hands to handle, grainy, sticky.

I have Grimm's honey, Grimm's fat.
A disturbed pool in the forest-clearing of my bowl.

It froths a beard at a small dark pane.

The knock of the axe, of the echo; the hum of flies,
and summer unwinding.

I add orange; add lemon zest.
I feel a charm twitch at the ends of my hands

of spice, its wisdom
of wooden seeds, of husks, carved bark, of bees in hovels
above the tracks of journeymen, red glass, skulking of shrews.

This dough has a well-travelled road.

Out there grows the blacker denser forest of the edge;
consists of lungs and guts and veins,
traces of dialect.

Sometimes an incident, domestic turmoil,
draws open space for solace

and we cry in that; our tears salt the dough.

Die-cut the shapes by which we figure
circles and hearts, and the fused shape of the human sacra.

Mature, after baking,
in a small sealed box, replacing at intervals

a thin slice of a locket (a heart) of apple.

Took one bitter radicchio
from garden frost,
washed of soil, slugs;
shredded the dampness.

To shorthand the phonetics of frying;
the faintness, the unfailing disturbed hiss
of sorting wetness from dryness:
a quick flash-heat bred for the scorch.

Hunger *is* spooky:
demand from under the diaphragm,
a small despot biting his fists.

The heat croaked,
the leaves turned vivid, bronze to bright green,

broke each scroll, the fortune of its palm.
Strange creeping technology, a leaf, as it wilts.

Added cream, lemon, scattered cheese,
its Latin dulcet, its Norse *tang*.
Tell, if it wasn't too bitter. . .maybe it was.
You ate rapidly, calmed – it was all right,
the year, flickering around us.

Under the electric light's fixed insidious glaze,
under the electric light's proportioning energy:
stripped mint
from the garden.

I inspect the spoil of its foliage (its creep, its light-work)
for insects, derelict bits of the shade.

It's potent, lying there gassing on the table;
it wakes, scent

chopped to a swarf: gathers its black oxides
to a bowl of apple, cucumber, yoghurt, green chilli. Stir
the bruised dream of mint.

As you touch (with your tongue)
the heated imprint of intuition
you will say *mint*. You will smell *mint*
in the net of your nerves.

I heat the pan. It happens quickly;
the cadence is furious.

Opalescence of oils disturbed with a rigid heat;
veiling flesh in a bodice of burns.
I work in batches, to sear the meat.

What an act of hospitality (this guest
lies in pieces, homeless).

Diana and Actaeon shrink apart.
I turn them together.
Red weeps in the cracks as I turn them over.
Segments congeal out of kilter, lean away.

I guide their enmity.

Quiet. I am doing this weird work
alone as a ranger of the dispossessed:
animal, nerves at hypnosis.
What is the trick?
What is the trick, what is the trick?
To keep spirit and meal wetly mixed.

The smoke is a rope rigging my work
to the year's light, and the distance.

Because I am Hestia, because you,
in passing, must be Hermes.
We, the dimensions humans exist in:
stuck and errant
(endless, peculiar transmission).

The smoke from the meat is in a dialogue –
down here to up there;
the struggle of gases and the years' tenuous, strange overlaps.

The smoke of deer-flesh: *how does it smell?*
Dry grass matted with blood, mud, pollen, urea.

It is all wound I cannot interpret;
a dislodged secret interior, only a part
I place at high heat,
to excite the rip-waste of sugars into ancient, charred shape.

Its melt-prints fuse
on the floor of the pan.

They wanted gratin.

I found potatoes
and the carefree of surplus milk;
I washed the potatoes
in the shadows of water.

Peeled, sliced, and layered
a scatter of onion, slices;

like the photons
Persephone unpicked from the loom each morning.

Could you do this? I washed the potatoes
in the water's shadows.

No crisis, as such, for the rest of the day. Just
a kitchen's criss-cross of paths,
the pounding, broad and interred
pain across ribs, the impending goodbyes.

I cut the potatoes. Nostalgia, I swear,
is homebound. Is bread. Is water's hardness.

Poured milk
across the shingles, the scales of potatoes.
(Its cooking played the fret-board of an hour;
in the clock's mechanics of metamorphosis.)

It came from the oven in a blistered skin,
liquids bubbling.
One of us served it; light turning grey,
it was that kind of evening. *Light turning grey.*

We were hungry; and ate
with our separate appetites –

[*I saw, in the dish, strands of onion*]

the lines of a body
in a body's rubble.

Black, green, rough in corrugations.

I cut a leaf on the wooden board,
strip it of all sleeves, clothes, its creaky panels
from its wristbone scaffolding,
stubborn, uncookable cellulose.

And release
from the totem of your winged head: *yours*.

Tried raw, I get
a mineral and Balkan windswept residual war-zone;
I get
a guard with rubber boots marching across the tongue.

I reckon
the clay, chapped stones, houses, are all empty.
I get
a mechanistic and bluff trace of smoke,
a bent crane under cracked paint.

A place without name, here, today to be eaten;
and in so doing
we cross your country, kale,
tripping on the verge onto the road through your fields.

The first cut goes into the inside,
the scene of the *in*;
the eternal wanderer reflected in water,
reflected in guts.

The second cut goes into the pallor,
something like the sweat after a murder;
hear
the small voice of a grill switched on.

The third cut I forget;
incised when the multitude began,
and was more like a sum.

The fourth cut is clean in half,
only for those too large to be one.

I picked the rained-on leaves
of the blackcurrant.

When they go
into the cream
it's like the cream has heard.

When I strain off
the ruined leaves
it's like the heat of a body
left in a bed.

Peeled, and halved, pears oxidise in minutes;

their tenable, brief overlap with our lifetimes' bodies.

I disassembled the gear of the cores, the innards;

took twelve threads of Spanish saffron
– immaculate, weird hair coral –
wove them at random
into the hot tapestry of boiled water.

They began their bleed,
licking the light through water about them:
a dye running red
into a portrait, a dedicating stain.

I crushed cardamom's resinous background.

In the prattling water, poached, half-bellied pears
absorbed a residual taste of eastern light.

[*Remove fruit, add sugar, reduce a syrup.*]

The vapours climbed unsteadily – through the existence of air,
vagrant and stray.

The fish arrives – it is the first bream
(stateless).
All day it rests dead in the fridge.

Baked now and hot and changed,
veins spiderweb the sweet white flakes
of the flesh under the foil;
(the face of the moon on the face of the water).
Boys sit in the fishy steam, wait to begin.

How mesmerising, how
painstakingly brought in on the black tray;
it appears alone in this world, like a void.

[*To cut, strike downwards from the bone.*]

They are amazed. From a family before,
to a family after:
seeing the mouth small in the context of body,
serrations of teeth jag the line of its area.

And here is the comb of the spine,
and there are bones like bodkins.

How it flickers.
How it flickers in the light we govern under.
Vigil and ache, temptation and now –

our present next to the dark;
next to the freak show of a meal's curio
trawled from the sea

(from fish-shaped rooms,
lost in the thickness and pressure of water below water).

Along the shores of our stomachs
we watch
and the single figure holds us
wrapped in its dark coverlet.

We leave just salvage, the boat's ribs.

Fry this in the black frying pan
with the low sides;
flip the image over its edge
as it sets,
hold
at the fire of skill
where the hearth continues;
the hearth is *holistic*,
I click to its magnet.
Where is my door, my other path?

Catch the flour with egg and milk;
all that I have on the non-stick of fat;
to flip,
and the year
turns on its shoulders:
a disc, in the flip
mid-air in the grace
of weakening resistance
to a fall.

(In the flip
I see the aperture
widen and fix
in air.)

And eat, once it's landed;
dole out to others
the others I make.

Will you fast?
We will fast tomorrow.

I feel a pale fatigue,
like the rough line in metal
which has bent too much.

Today I work
for the opened mouth.

Picked wild garlic;
the green leaves we smashed,
bulbs and roots veiled in the rootline;
suspension of shreds in slime.

You would see a screech owl's carcass;
the leathery palm of a liver,
the green-black smear of a gall-bladder.

You would see the bulbs like molars
in the red earth;
clumps of garlic in shadows along the scarp.

Half way along, you would feel the draught:
Come in to the shadow of colder earth.

Why would we eat this?
It is a bride, they say.
Disgusting. And it would be
if we did not disguise the stubborn knee-jerk perfume.

I made a jug of its liquid suspension.
Added salt, oil, pine-nuts, parmesan.

It was rank, as the alloyed mixture bubbled
and weirds frothed almost a speech:

I'm ashamed you've seen me like this,
as it heated the windpipe, watered the eyes.

We used it again, and again, and again.

And each time, remembered how the vapour
had burst from the pounded leaves
as Medea at the end of her crimes
flew up
into her own sentence, and by word vanished.

Today, dropped artichokes
into brine to sit for an hour.
Weighed down under the heavy plate,
three earwigs struggled to be buoyant.

Humans flare from their soils.
So bring to the boil,
the nudged, grey, inner sanctum
of the flower.

The water is black, the eaters wait:
staring,
sat in the trees of their nerves
like rooks.

So that the fibres relax, after cooking –
its vapours light-footed –
I have set it to rest on a board on the side;

and you come – meat eaters –
various swift and busy, from far away,
to this attraction emitting its curious signal.

And if I stand apart
I catch your half-livid reverence:
bright-eyed, dark-mouthed.

It is ready to carve.

I have the madness (of Heracles) to worry me.
I serve (his) somewhat ecstatic children.
Under each breath, its coil pulls all of us in.

They are dying, really dying
in the water washing them.

Do not rough-handle, go delicately;
It's like bodies: just the skin,
a refracted stage lifting an image
out of the house's prism,
leaving this spareness to conduct,
as I
turn the wheel of the tap and see
how they have grown small:
pure of weight, pure of mass.

What is the grammar of leaves?

This curly fan I tear into pieces, is endive, for example,
thin, wet wasting sunlight; its bitter participle.

I dip and shake;
the whole world of its time flickers on and off.

Tear, not chop.

(And I heard through broken conversation:)

And everything's been violated, you said.
And everything's been mixed, I said.
I saw the objective of salad, *it is no one place,*
it is no one place.

How long have you been in this house
stirring, washing degrees of stasis?
It is not tedious, there is no stasis.

And if you see your lettuce like I see this,
for what it is,
some groomed with a red like the burnish on copper
when a bearing has worn down, or a buckle, part-perished,
has some function of wear to it;

a strange temperature,
neither human nor predator.

And it's a frail copy of the sun's hours, a likeness
you put to your ear (like I have my ear
to the skin of this weak infinite risk),

and you find it's of a kind of leaf
very closely attenuated with your failure
to kill it and keep it –

like the Titans, the giants,
when they came into the mirror,
ashen,
and killed the body (*of this*) for the heart.

• KIPPER •

I sit (alone) at this incident of supper;
all others are out
and the house has the tilted feel of a deck.
I have a kipper dyed with the trace of smoke
in the grime of the room.
I will eat its processed pieces.
Cut open are its two heads,
its hook, hole, flesh, eye, fins, translucent lips,
all the marks and the bones and scales,
a circuitry of scorched components;
glass bones of whisker dewed with oil.
But in this cave of the kitchen painted darkly
the kipper is bright like a still life would be lit;
no one about to disturb its
quiet, arranged mass
of empty spaces under the colours.
Hours of attention I reduce to minutes
of dribbles and scrapes and a slow make-do
turning and lowering it into milk;
its miracle an ordinary, viable type:
fish inlaid into my home,
into my flesh too, its feedings.
Remove from the milk's simmer.
I have poached it in milk.
The butter I touch on it melts;
butterness glazes in platelets of yellow,
a tortured ochre, sienna, a carotene,
a dismal scorched edge;
its innards' pink alabaster flakes,
glints in its eyes' inset obsidian;
its animal mouth of fretsaw teeth.
Its rich flesh torchlights my body with heat,
its grave totality keeps me arrested.
The trawlers moving towards dawn's grim sweep,

trawlers like trawlers in a storm or a film
about fishing and work,
or fishing and danger, or the dead and heroes.
Its horizon-in-progress flickers,
a thin, primrose line of daylight,
a tear in the night's wall,
and the small boat flowing back to harbour
with the fished and foreign,
the figurines of men.
And fish; flashing bright bullion of water,
hurting and gasping into a writhing bale.
The butter pools over;
I taste the ruined cartography of smoulder;
see the knife-blade mark and wound-size of its length;
the cold stain of its smokehouse life,
nearly Neolithic bog-grave remains.
I pick through its flesh's embers,
the milk-smoke fog of its flakes;
the anatomy litters on the purse of its skin,
its loose stocking-silk sequinned.
The odour of its oils,
the two, hinged boards of its symmetry;
bones which could choke.
I look down from above,
craned over the deck,
at the caught shoal's
flicker of fish, bright
and netted, under the bow shudder, the keel-lean.
All hollow, holy objects: boats.
And tilt my head through the vapours
rising off the one dead fish on the plate.
Its salt taste, its stink, will seep in my fathoms,
a mutilated, dream creature,
fish woman of canoe ribs who arrives
and keeps me,
detailed with her rough bone head's eyes,

jutting mouth with its silver lip,
the harp of her bones.
We merge:
our cell is unlit; our bed, black.
But I drop the plate, as I rise
and kneeling to clear it:
fuck this mess…
What is that face on the floor,
its pale reflecting slipper of light…
this long hard thinking about a death…
What is that face
of fish bone and spilt milk and skin
looking up like it's known me? So blue.
What have I eaten?
Was it male or female?
I said to its phantom, *go, go away*.
But it will not,
it has not.
What have I eaten?
What am I made of? What am I?

On the third day
we visit the brewery's basin:
a scud of froth;
emerging tone of beer.

The room has soured, it has a breath
like it's been up sucking rotten apples all night.

The darkened flowers appear repentant,
serving the yeast;
its cloudy depth the frog pond,
the festering depth
where the dead float.
You wouldn't swim there.

Six hours and six hours and six hours and six hours pass –

the brew bristles on
through the scales of thunder.

A divined, accelerated chaos
controlled as fire. [*Stir, and re-cover.*]

Four hours we stole out of and came back
to its prickling spirit.

It is a green hue of secret,
the ingredients foetal;
fatally, we rear the alter ego, the monster
human of the tree.

I stare at the oracle of the brewery.
So much is slow.

Silenus
I think you should have never entered this room.

I instruct you to test by spoon,
and if so, if right, decant and strain its incantation.
Done.
And between the veils of your palms
hold the bowl, its streamer slipping steadily to light.
Done.
And listen: the burping has held you still.

Petals, ruffs, a small slime
dredged on the sieve: a pulp of rags;
swarf of its flowers.

So the liquid goes
and twists through the Styx of the bottleneck
like it's a reason
to forget the common of sense
and to grow bodily and wholly dysfunctional.

I lean on the minutes;
lick of pale fat; the hiss of melting.

This image of me, before the fire,
bartering with Hades –
taking light from the shadows

[*energy of plants, the fuel of sugars*].

This is the toast:
honey pours through its holes;

I let dogs through a forest.

Its calories will burn
(glow-worm light)
in skulls, tonight;

under the hair of children,
in the lamps of brains.

To have something unstoppable struggling for breath,

like it's leaning, mocked
at midday, among the weeds,
the popping bubbles;

the beery, associated belches,
off-guards, odd-bods;

like late at night under a strip-lamp
on an empty train, you undress your principles

and expose the constant of *you* rummaging through perception
for an exit.

And I am shivering, sick, unsteady and harmless.

To ache and decline and stir slowly away;

to trail through a soft-footed melancholia
spilling a dripping spoor of slur, a vomit of meanings:

the odd incised, isolated real truth that comes bobbing up
and surprises the flash wit of a room,

like a fish leaps out of nothing into less

with the full contents of a bottle or two,
and the day lengthening

into that caught feeling
in the ribs, like brash, like flood, debris, high and
inarticulate, hanged in the minutes of your outer life.

Quick bitter growth, face irregular, flies on chin,

caught fishing without a licence
for the lumens, the light of a dead object;

a fish, its performance of death,
its belly bloated

under the light of flowers, in the water of flesh.
I saw a fish. I fell in fishing.

How milk jellifies, oddly recalcitrant,
on adding this enzyme.

Touched with a spoon-end, it splits, sinister:
a thin yellow whey gives barely a taste.
We blindly trust its separation – it tastes of salt.

Has no mouth, no eye – only a duality of innards.

Night, and I cut the lake of this junket.
Its singular flesh is very pale
and splits again
into something to offset the qualm of illness.

A sad bowl of milk,
as in the inertia of spooning to an invalid –
chin jut, head tilt back, the mouth's cup.

Very old child, toothless, ambulance for milk's ghost;

so bleakly bodily
so mute like a door knocker
wrapped in cloth.

Has this feel of shedding time,
the stray vague loom of a dawn's vapour.
It is doctored milk –
we swallow its curse.

First, to acidify the body of milk:
a drop of lemon.

Like the sun coagulating morning:
dense fogs drift

and there are the granular objects of daylight:
things to fight, to negotiate.
I watch it weave its apparitions.

Add enzyme.
Its rite has no blood, no breath.

And here, like a miracle of Canaan,
it turns through obedience to hypnosis
into something civil.
And the curd, and the whey,
they uncollect from the unity of milk.

And we have our lesson:
a sudden set work – milk's medium evicting each of its parts.
I see Abel and Cain, arthritic,
holding silent, staring the stare.

Take hold very gently
with spoons or hands.

[*Keep the whey, its slippage,
to cool for pigs, or to cook.*]

The gentlest of violations,
all bodies taint it.

Your touch must be motherly.

Handling its newborn, dripping, first minutes,
we are a picture; not a spare taste,
nothing to name yet.
And us, effort, manually depicting process
grow archaic, almost historic.

With spoons
winding each ball of elastic instinct,
foetus, pre-bones, making tenuous decisions for it,
narrowing its pulse and fixing a person

we search with the eyes of Tiresias,
a sort of grey ultrasound
through flesh's clouds into its privacy,
and there: the human in the invasion.

Sirens, traffic, poverty are sores across it.
This curd is a man with malnutrition

we learn to salt, drain, press,
and wrap in muslin, like its last rites
growing its own smell, its own corpse
we roll the stone across.

… and pour this cord of oil converse to the earth's spin;
towards the violence of the earth's turning,

to the hot pan's floor, the cold-pressed oil
from Jerusalem's groves or modern Greece;

and if there's any wetness, or damp, or, like rain,
it's like a flash of breaking glass, very thin,
smashed up from below.

The cord is umbilical from the bottle's mouth:

in the o of the pan,
its echo of vertigo heats, till smoke wavers, thin,
into the echo of air.

The fluid floor of the pan grows scribbled
hot – jumpy, alert
like a tool – a value – prone to fire …

Made bread, the quick method;
found beatification, in yeast, water;
its mealy ecstatic.

Its deep law, the whole kitchen
virtuous with bread-dough's proving.

Knocked back its coarse gold,
its risen ingot flecked with the bran.

Turned and folded and pressed-down its clean turmoil;
the gluten contracted into a body;
we shaped and scored – you drew with the knife.

Baked rid of its passion,
a feral colour reddened the crust – *a feral redness.*

I saw the rudiment,
forty minutes of the oven's derangement of matter.

It tapped hollow; we cleaned the bowl, ate bread.

How new it tasted;
the body of grass, darkened into us.

In batches we seal the oxtail pieces.
Minutes pass.

And what a mirage flavour is,
all down the end-sections of the ox's brain.

Drowned in red wine, bay, thyme,
every twist and dead end, and turn
under the wreath's crown
of hurt, long, dark sanctuary of the herbs we use.

We salivate too, now it is no longer distant
but a calm we temper with,
the estuarine slow movement over the earth
of cattle.

This is the hut of our time, it spans generations:
in smoke walls,
a fume's roof canvas pitched
over stewing beefstock.
We dispatch ideas into ordinary life;
we stand in our agriculture.

All day is the simmer and the browning of stew.
Now nightfall, it falls off the bone.

Plate, *clink*, divide between bowls; nearly elegant,
the strange matter of vertebra
perplexing, prehistoric; they appear as we eat
out of stew-tide liquor,
the blocks of the spine, all up our core –
we have those too.

Stand in compressions of winter
like that woman in the shadow who keeps the light alight
at this dark time in the North;
mix song and fairytale,
and blood, blood's taste,
the iron residual in dried fruit,
planets of glacé cherries,
pegs of suet;
throw the flat moon with the dead king's head
to the pudding's lump deep.
Stout is in, Hesperides' incurable dark;
Gawain's smell of boozy breath,
the knights in the dead wood (in essence)
at his lord's high table.

Beans, I kept
– like a killer keeps a corpse –
in the freezer five months;

loosened to scalding depth,
rattled through a drum of venting oxygen:
I serve forkfuls of hot, bright pulse.

To five yolks, add granulated sugar.
Beat to a stiff, translucent putty, which tightens
to a tone relaxing from the pressure
of the spoon. [*Used human power.*]

Custard *is* nursery-ingredients
at the brood-end of flesh.
Only the sugar's mechanically-laboured

(pain excised from the edge of Africa).

But how good, how earth-like,
to take these baked damsons
(to disintegrate into *us*, in our stomachs).

Brought cream to the boil;
to pour to the bowl
we use to bind custard (its inside slink).
The thin crinkled skin lifted off like a caul.

Whisked warm into the yellow yolk-sugar;
its basin set in the simmering inch.
Not a speed but a slurring constant
at the heavy pan's loiter, obeying towards thickening.

Bring damsons de-stoned, and skinned, the pulp.

Combine, cool, and freeze

to a paralysis of inhabitants; the stopped
flow which splinters to crystal;
an itch we smash at two-hour intervals;
freeing its teeth back to glitter.

[*Months go by.*] It still tastes specific:
of homestead phenomena, the forest-road's lay-by.

I was washing up, when
an owl flew to the window
(this kitchen window)

and grew the splay of its fan;
a pale halo of wingspan,
white and eerie; the traveller

or a similar apparition, caught partially;
I remember it all.

The hour grave; I lurked in the form
of what a human is, stooped over cleaning
utensils, disorder;

pressed to a mouse-fear at the back of me,
a tenure in doom; astonished at the pull
of this predator: every feather and claw,

the detailed grease-print
on the glass and my own, living, tensed light.

It has shaken off its own anatomy
into outer minutiae.

I thought, to get glass clean: vinegar.

I remember it all:
    it squeaked like shrews
being killed
as I polished the owl away.

And against my own reflection on the black, dark night,
I continued to scour
the film off crockery –
 rinsing the suds,
perfecting the gleam.

• OLD BREAD FOR BREAD PUDDING (TO PREPARE) •

I work at the edge of the edible;

remains of bread
at the grey end of domestic detail.

A wheaten figure we tore together;
genetics broken;

various pieces,
various scraps

of another life;

its grey old sponge serenely drinks,

soaking away;

the loops of its hours,
stirred and let be.

• BURNT BREAD •

I have burnt the bread.

Out of oven-amnesia
comes its creaky, aerated block;
fired and vitreous;
its incinerated wetness, its weight.

But,
if you could be lifted into a light corpse,
like this,
it would be a means of going on
– only – as carbon.

The brain's pattern, full of its intricate location
– all models of event, all issues of space and time –
recorded to its dark lexicon.

I lift its portable, black artefact.
It floats (like a suspect, floats like a woman
in the seventeenth century);
exceeds
all the cookery of the mortal.

Begin, rinsing foods we do not eat:
onion skin, broccoli stems, parsley stalks.

They drown factually, cooking; unreal green.

I push a chicken's carcass underneath [*simmer gently,*
for clearer juice];
the long neck-bit, the giblets. Peppercorns, whole. A clove, or two.

Not grey, but a weak winter-field-gold
is what I aim for;
like when the ground is cold, and the sun walks
through the day's armour and disarray.
[*Could use as a soup's lace, for instance.*]

Note this for character, in a stock –
the bones old, thin, brittle flutes empty of marrow,
gossamer parts of the meat,
its muscular garments reduced to thread.

Strained and cooled, it grows close to glue –
set, tapped, quaking, intact (under its lid of yellow fat).

Damsons, gathered and washed;
and my heartbeat, whenever I stopped,
rocked me quite furiously, back and forth.

The day was a wound of wet red robes
stained carmine by matchlight;

this wet flaxen flesh; juice running free, abused by the air;

a dark slowing of time,
now that the day was ending –
north light, bastard light,
and everything quite quiet,
except for my hands scrabbling.

Two and a half pounds of weight
I measured of the flesh;

simmered until it had softened,
bog-like; the marvellous glimmer
I pressed through the sieve,
extracting its blood, its red juice.

From the pulp I took the wet stones
– I could hear my breathing's tremor –
a tricky but ordinary task,
to crack the stone of a damson.
You can fail, I muttered, to myself.
Dangerous in ways, too, to fail to oneself.

Hands a dun, grey colour. Astringent – I think,
the word – that makes skin tighten, like this.

The pan was a black lake:
twenty or so stones, in the end…
at what might be a shore, a place,
to kneel and extract

(from slick, harried parts of a violation).

Each stone opened like a wooden womb
or a small sarcophagus;
the vision – very mute, nevertheless –
of the small pip, quite naked, pale:
two white foetal feet pressed sole to sole over each sought tree.

It was effort,
pressing the weave of the sieve
over barren gloom, the spoon rummaging
the spoon-back rite, for stones in the pulp.

[*Very low-grade ritual.*]

Worked at the ratio one to one, with sugar;
brought the thrash of the boil;
pressured the skin of its froth
like you would stir down into time's worry,
its troubles, its commune, its killing area.

Almost involuntary,
as the liquid thickened, it lifted a torus of gas.

Somewhere I saw
the division in the spectrum
between the horse and the man of a Centaur,

like in the waterline at boil-point,
like, in the search
between water and steaming self,
was the scar's other story.

I was stirring when he came here,
leaning as I am now towards my future;
boiling is a vexing bumping of bodies.
As I was stirring, he entered
with the body of a gift: Here, he said,
holding it out.
What is your journey?
The long road with the dusty dead.
Convening memories; fragile, eroded animals.
He stood, loitering, awkward, long-haired.
It was a chalky light he carried in, on his skin.
I stood in the noise of transition by fire.
Our mutual arena was so very short-lived.
Come here, closer. He came
and touched my hair with his rough face;
my ear with damaged words. I sensed
a clear, small miracle was being carried
under the depth of language.
You are not dusty, like the others, he said.
Benevolent, or scared, or very calm,
he unwrapped a small plastic tub,
unwrapped a fillet of pale meat.
The nets of his eyes in disrepair.
Come here, I said, and I pressed his eyes shut,
brief-lived shut-eye, rested his head,
and said, *all vision is attempted flight.*
I went to the fire; I seared the flesh
of the animal he'd brought. As he went
I caught sight
of the long scar, as he shut the door.

I pull the still, dark fibres of the mutton
(the house is quiet);
the cooked, long bone of the upper leg
(the house is quiet);
the mute, incontestable fact
of a creature standing, by itself.

Its tallow is cold, blind, dormant, quick to melt.

Come in: the room is quiet.

Could burn it for light, this tallow.
How would it smoke, fling shape, flick shadow
bigger than us
through this house.

The house is very quiet. Tonight,

we would kill the shadows for the shadow of blood,
out of the light from burning fat;
would puncture the shadows for the shadow of blood,
like Sebastian and his arrows.

Hold bright leaves of November's chard,
the river of the tap, shut;

plunge hands and shake off rattling drips,
loose silt and grit.

Its tin-helmet green,
its scarlet and dark
shivers through tightened seconds
right up into the clothes of the present;

where I am born, older,
lifting the limp, unwieldy
twist of its pressure,
of leaf and leaf, and leaf –

The high voices outside are coming in;
to turn over the first taste of leaves.

I am watching, from a little way off
– I make myself watch their fleeting minute –
the barely candescent
childhood – time of children

– look, so little light is needed to light them –

they run in their bodies;
come in
to the family
of water falling, of air in leaves;

it almost has unity – a relay of futures'
contact with the uncanny flash of water:

water I washed with, cooked in, washed in;
water they ate, water they drank.

We stir … and the room's content
swings through the mixture.

The wooden spoon
paddles centre-stage,
a slow whirlpool of generations

deep in the hurtling house:
its complex; its time; its trance.

I see you … children … add your belief,
your wishes, your prayer, your guess,

under the small shower of electric light
in winter's massive, dark coagulate.

I do not know what will stay in
the cake as it cooks:

if the year, through the spoon's turn,
or the years, if they are there,
if they *will be* there
when the skewer comes out clean.

• CUSTARD •

Beat egg-yolks into sugar,
whisk into hot milk.

This *is* craft,
fitting the feverish project of flame

to a binding so child-like
a resolution takes place,

clings to the back of a spoon.

A fine line between
possession of fortune,
possession of failing.

I cut, for sealing jams
brown post-office packing paper,
draw round a lid for size.

One day, two years away, I imagine
these older fingers
will take down this pound of weight's changed character;

and who will know anyone there?

I am about to begin again
psychoanalysis of substance; a second batch

bringing fruit and sugar into the marriage of oddness.

This jam on the boil is a puzzle,
a pond throwing out scalds;

its aptitude: a thing quite unintentionally
able to go transformed,

because this is the anatomy you get, the syrup

as it bulks down losing the looseness of a life,
its sugars bend into a suspension; look,
I have made a hiatus.

It is not unkind to render a body clean,
to keep life after life in a calm
under blank dials of brown paper;

the jelly cools, sucks airless, free of taint,
the whole of time slows to a single spasm.

(Odd taxidermy; in the glass jar's thorax:
the fruit's animal, its death.)

But not the hunger of Solzhenitsyn,
not the bread-ache of the clutched-in mouth,
but our own prevailing grip of cold
killing the garden's vegetables: all struggle to survive.
Lorries with foodstuffs pass us.
We eke out silence between their passages.
We walk the impoverishing glitter of frost,
poking for roots the mice have taken.
I stay, making steam out of soup this morning.
Our bread is a little curled up.
But, it's good to eat this together.
We hear the wind under the door upstairs
through the quiet repeating reflex of sips.
The children are gone.
And when the table's cleared, we go our ways
through the rest of daylight.

Where was I?
Reducing a language.

Take apples, these, full simmer,
the fluid feel of the stir.

This minute's turning of existence
evolves out of my arm:

and *I am* disturbed by the sound of the simmer:
its unrest,
its undressed, butchered, de-cored disorder.

Burning fuel,
I feel the minutes of millions of years blur,
helix and disappear.

I swear it's what life is
here in *this* apple: a chopped, sliced silence
in audience with depth; none can dislodge
that active and malic oddness.

And how the air hurries, breathes, respires;
a head over the stove
hurts carefully, hearing
the lilt and tremolo
hiss
of the offering.

Windfalls have a discoloured flavour of ruthless earth.
Spiders spun in the looms of their mothers.

Bletted-by-heart, they shine when we wash them;
cut crosswise, the stars of pips.

Two years on
I will hold them high to see that
shrunken-from-the-jar
chrysalis of sugars.

Turn back the weeks:
old times hang about my work;
tasks in pre-mother tongue, of chores still resonant.

I have only a mind to cook with.
Cook, then, in your mind of things.

I hold a big spoon of beech wood.
And the preserving pan smells of cider;
a rough clamping vinegar;
an insolent, fraying society at work:
a bed of apples borne to a pulp.

And if I'm honest, they fall apart,
shrinking clothes, old leather jerkins
paring away;
apple that once was *the* apple.

I have its pool of heads as testimony;
a crimson I stoop at.

Set aside, before pulping and sieving;
I wonder
what will its new language be to begin with?
devoid of pip sheaths, skin rags, personae.
(I had a spoonful in the recess of my mouth,
but could not decode all of its flavour.)
Add one clove's staining unopened flower.

Incubated
in its glass calm, stored in the muffles
of larder dark,
I will bring it with cream and hazelnuts
to the haunted table:
old trick, old story, fabled winter dark,
the talk of absence, ghosts, toasts, under the light;
under the light
eat to absent futures, friends, the brethren woods.

• LEFTOVER •

I pick at a cold (cooked) fish-finger: its relic;
grip and slice
the black beach of the oven's yesterday,

mining for energy.
Disquiet; *why can't you leave it?*

How clammy it is, how tightly crusted.

A phantasmal hunger
spooks through our innards.

I take the morsel by mouth;
that waspish sawing theft,

that homestead's
dry sound of the tooth;

saying, here, *eat this. Be quiet with this.*

ACKNOWLEDGEMENTS

Thanks to Trinity College Cambridge for invaluable time and space, to the Society of Authors and Arts Council England for financial assistance, to family and friends who have in so many ways shaped these poems by living in and around them – for being at the table, for reading, listening, cooking, eating, talking; especial thanks to friends in Cambridge, to Angela Leighton, and to my editor Robin Robertson.

Acknowledgements are due to the editors of *Poetry Review*, *Poetry Ireland Review* and *PN Review*.

To Orlando and Louis, the cause of my keeping hearth – *Human Work* is for them.